159 CELTIC DESIGNS

Amy L. Lusebrink

DOVER PUBLICATIONS, INC.
Mineola, New York

For Septentria

PUBLISHER'S NOTE

Amy L. Lusebrink has rendered Celtic motifs that can be used directly on graphic or crafts projects or as a source of inspiration. The author has taken a broad interpretation (also including a few Gothic motifs that seemed related) in which the hallmarks of the style are represented: knotwork, keys, spirals and zoomorphic interlacements.

159 Celtic Designs, first published by Dover Publications, Inc., in 1993, is a republication of the illustrations originally published by Scotpress, Bruceton Mills, WV, in 1988 under the title *The Celtic Copy Book: Celtic Designs to Photocopy*. The text is here omitted.

Library of Congress Cataloging-in-Publication Data

Lusebrink, Amy L.
[Celtic copy book. Selections]
159 Celtic designs / Amy L. Lusebrink.
p. cm. — (Dover pictorial archive series)
Republication of the illustrations of: The Celtic copy book. Bruceton Mills, W. Va. : Scotpress, c 1988.
ISBN-13: 978-0-486-27688-5
ISBN-10: 0-486-27688-0
1. Decoration and ornament, Celtic—Themes, motives. I. Title. II. Title: One hundred fifty-nine Celtic designs. III. Series.
NK1264.L8725 1993
745.4'49415—dc20 93-10729
CIP

Printed in Canada
27688013 2025
www.doverpublications.com

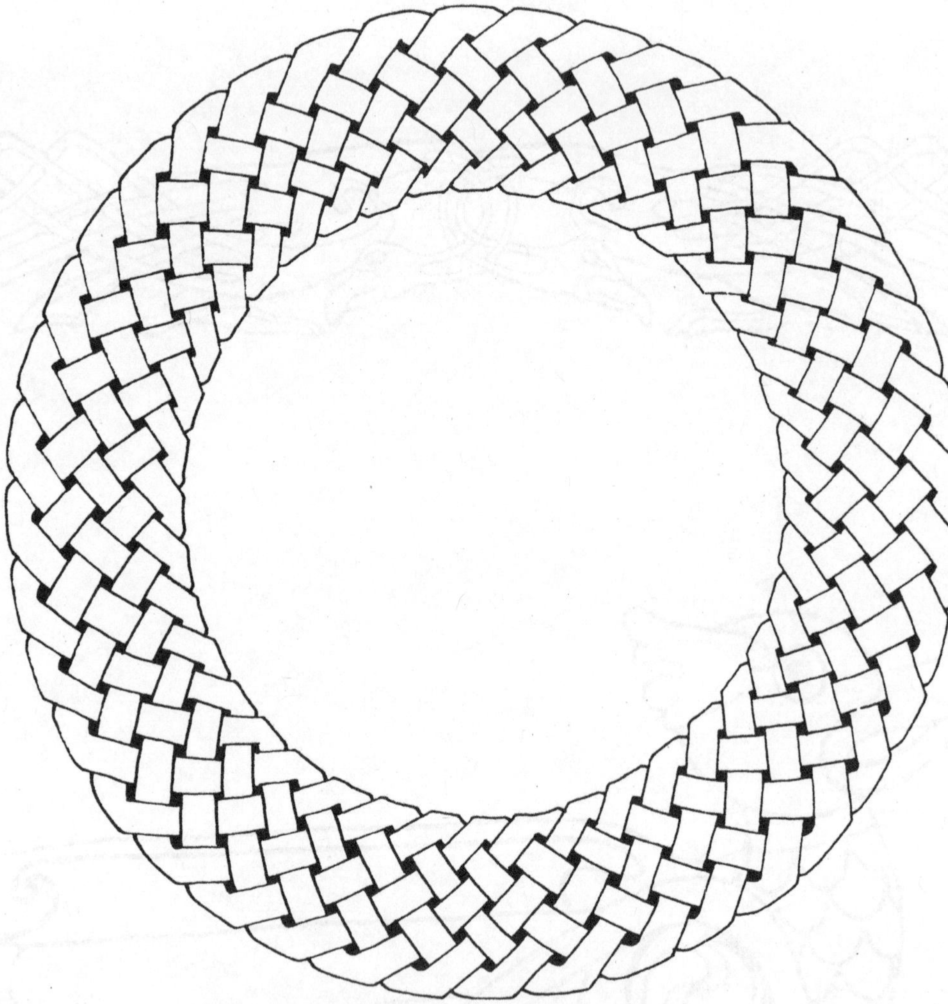

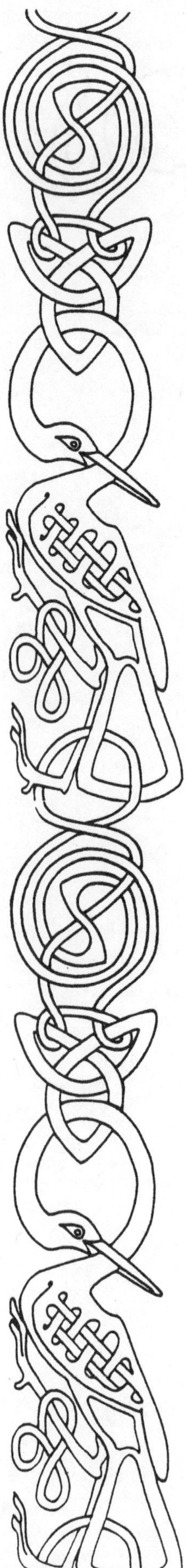

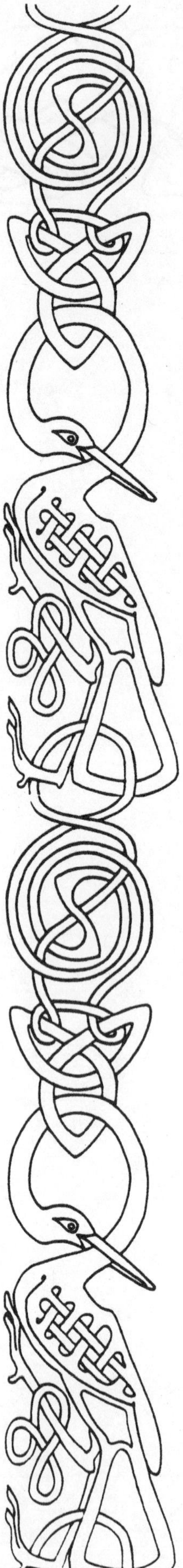

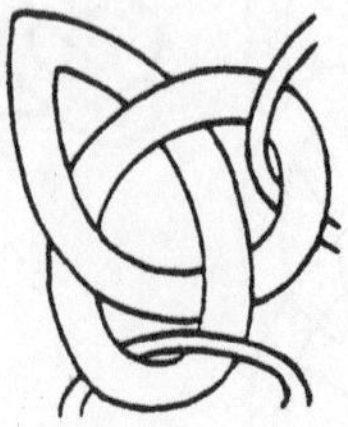

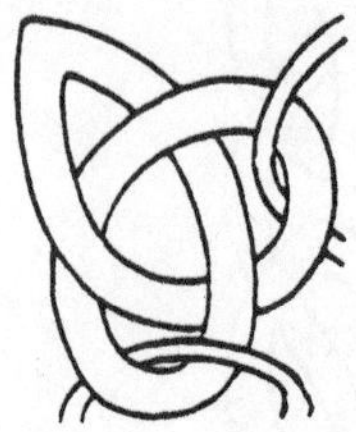

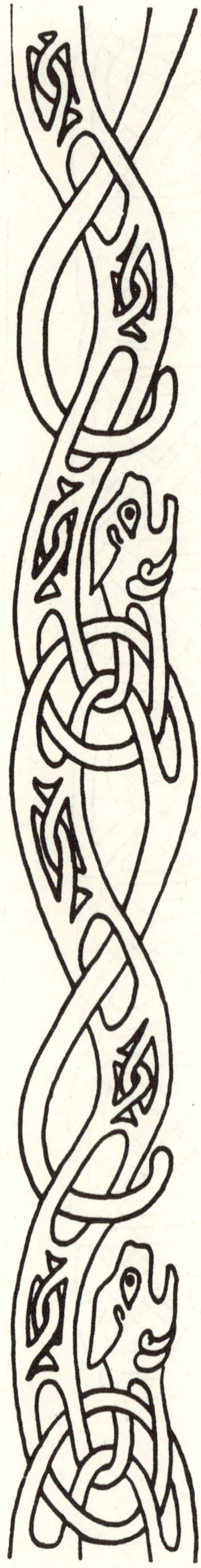

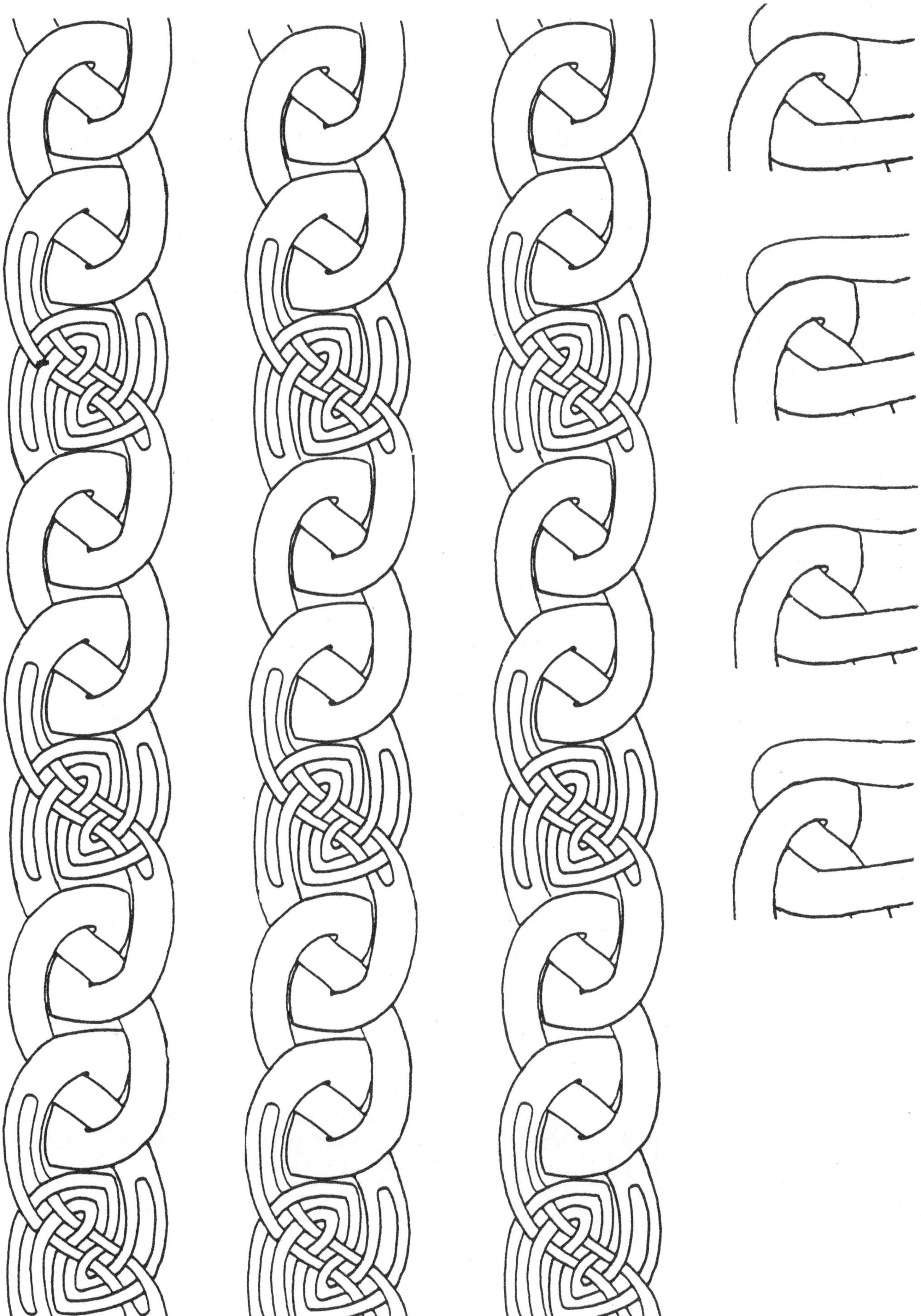

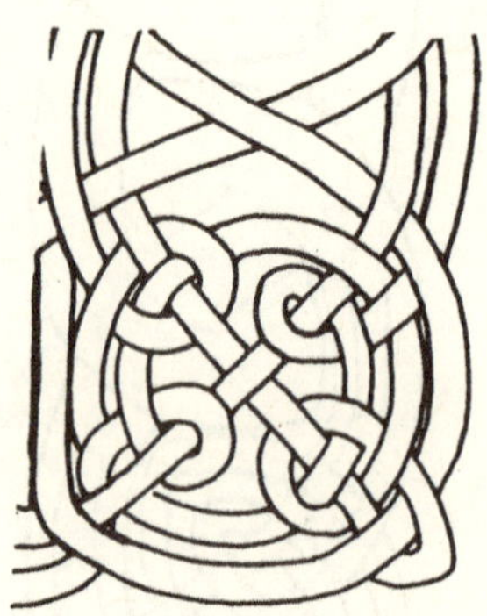

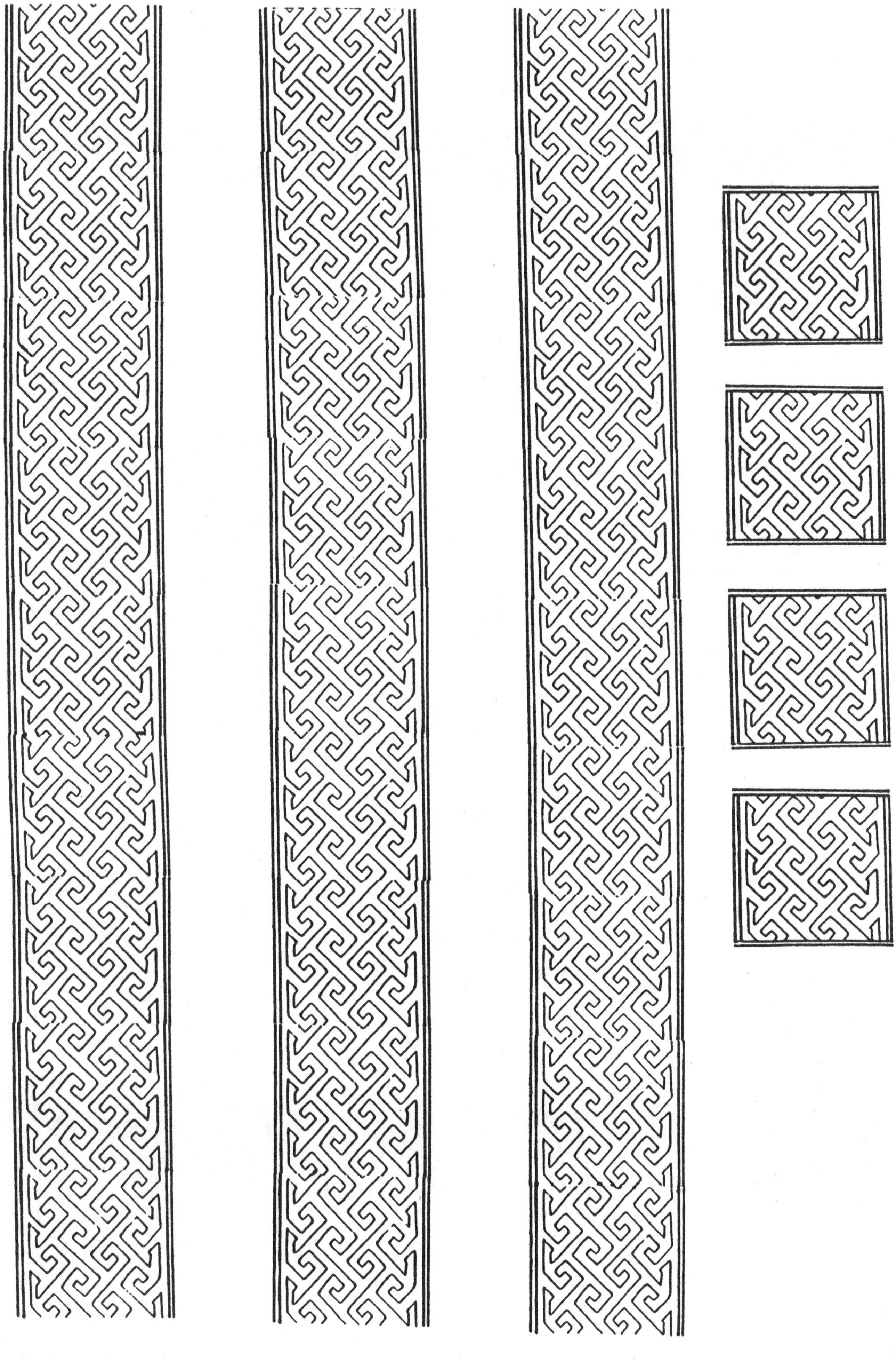

ab
cde
fgh

X Y
Z

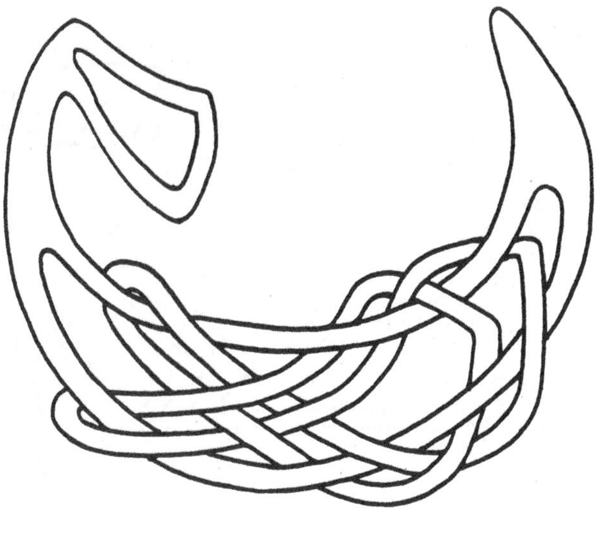
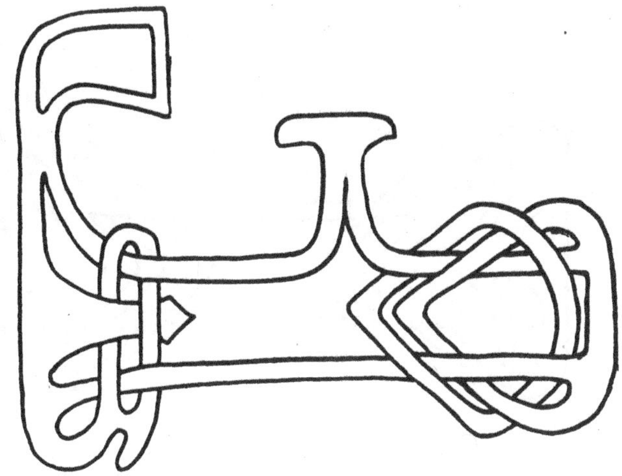

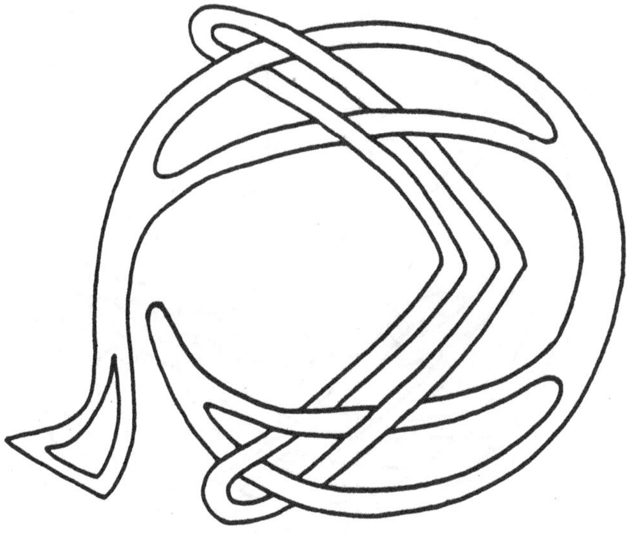

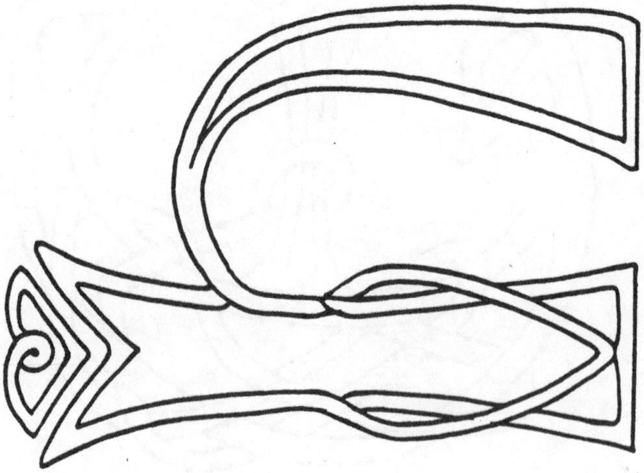

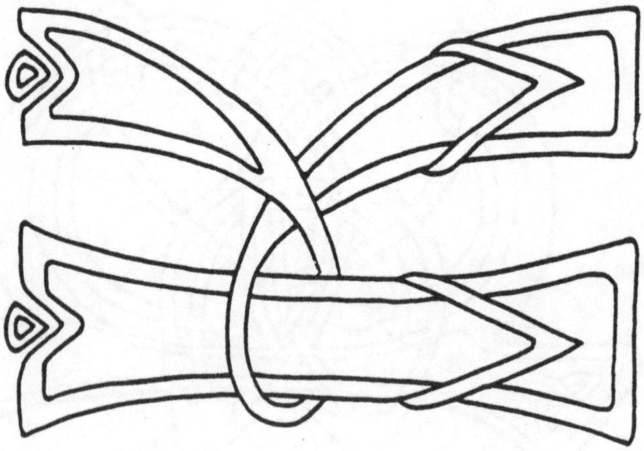

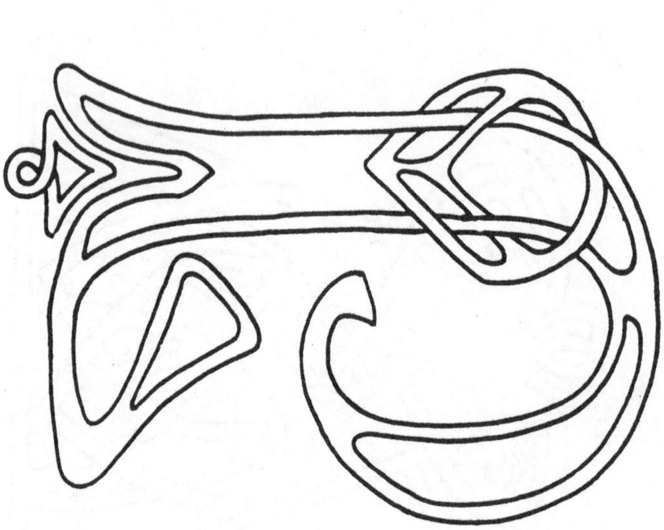

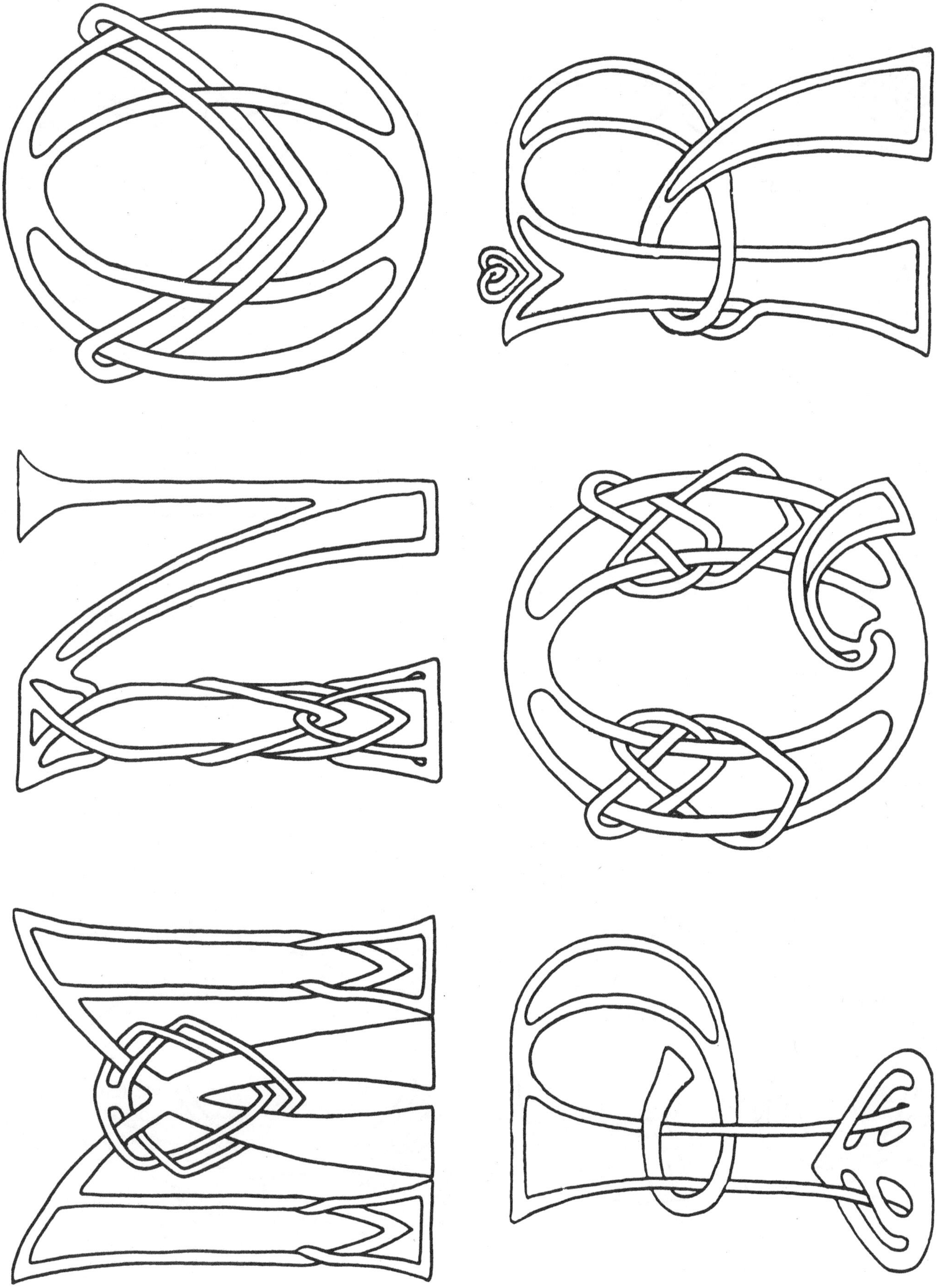

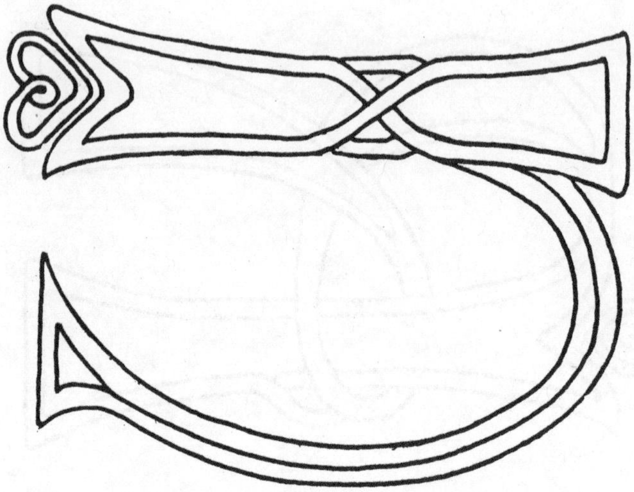

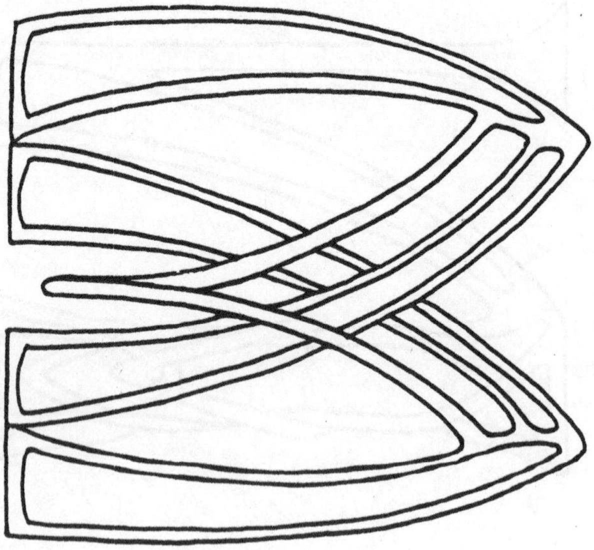
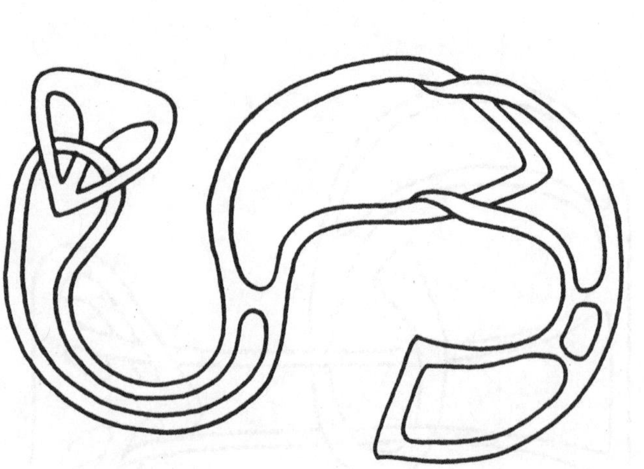

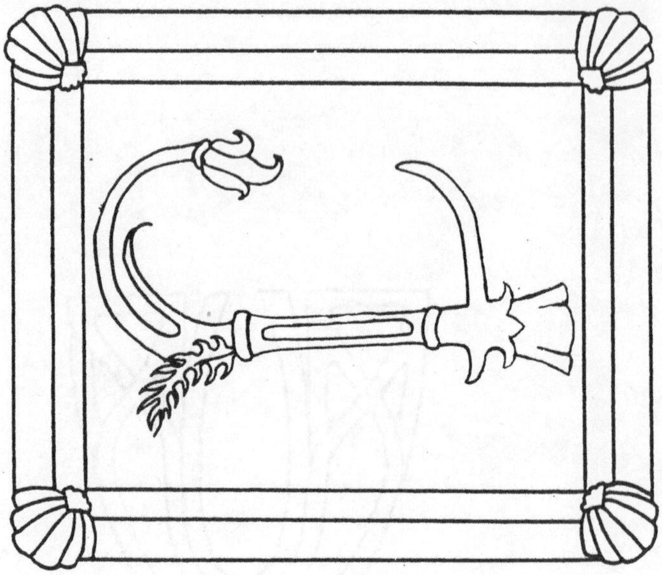

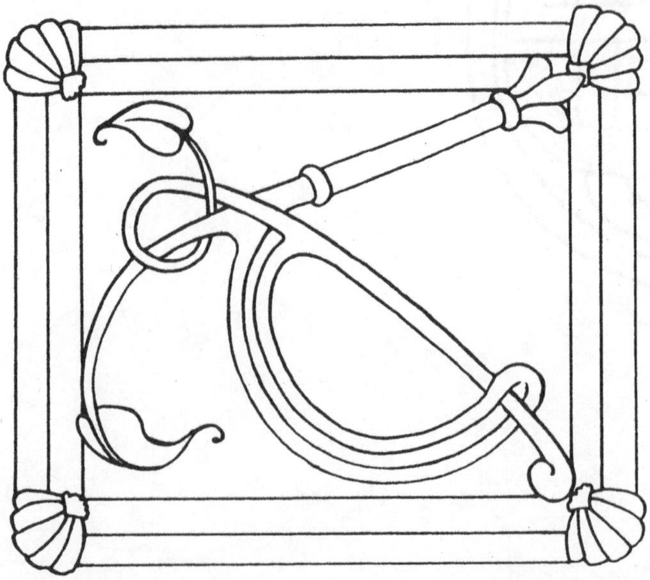

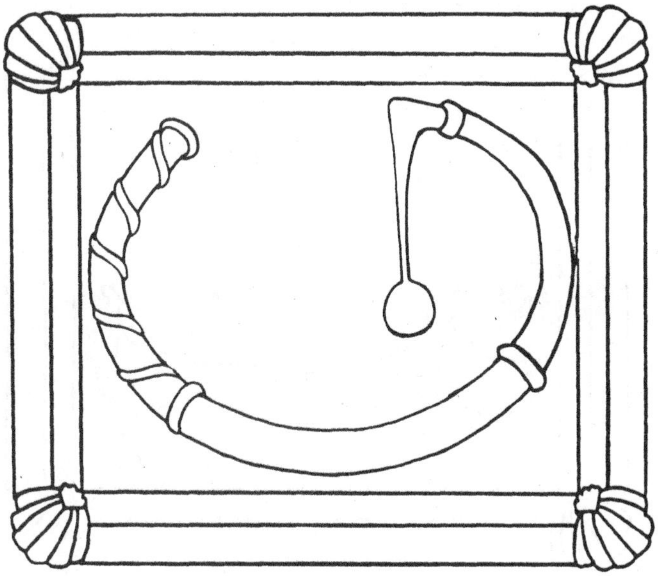
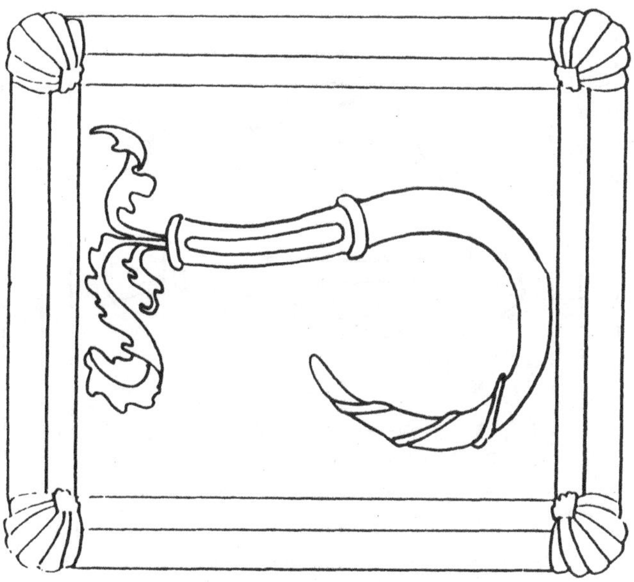

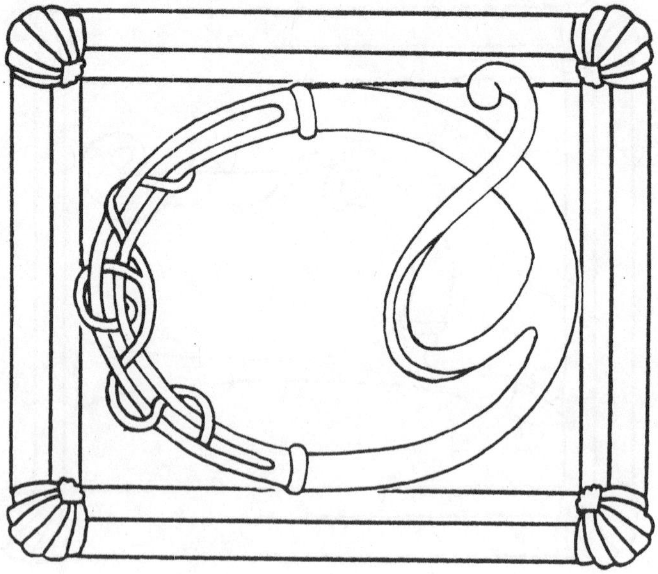

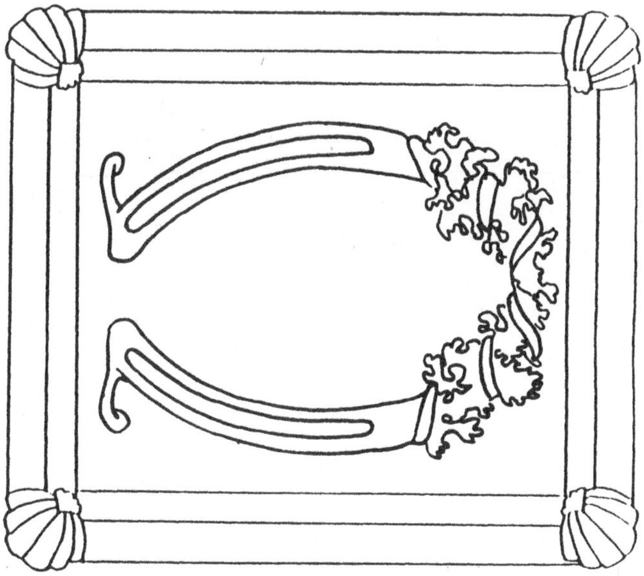

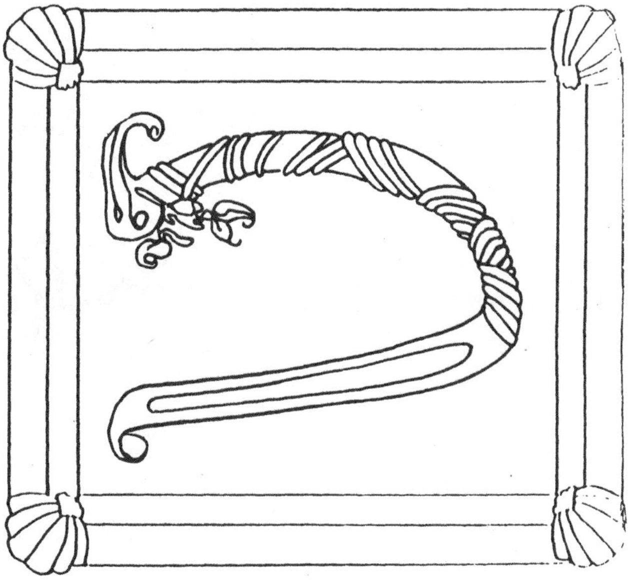

Y

Z

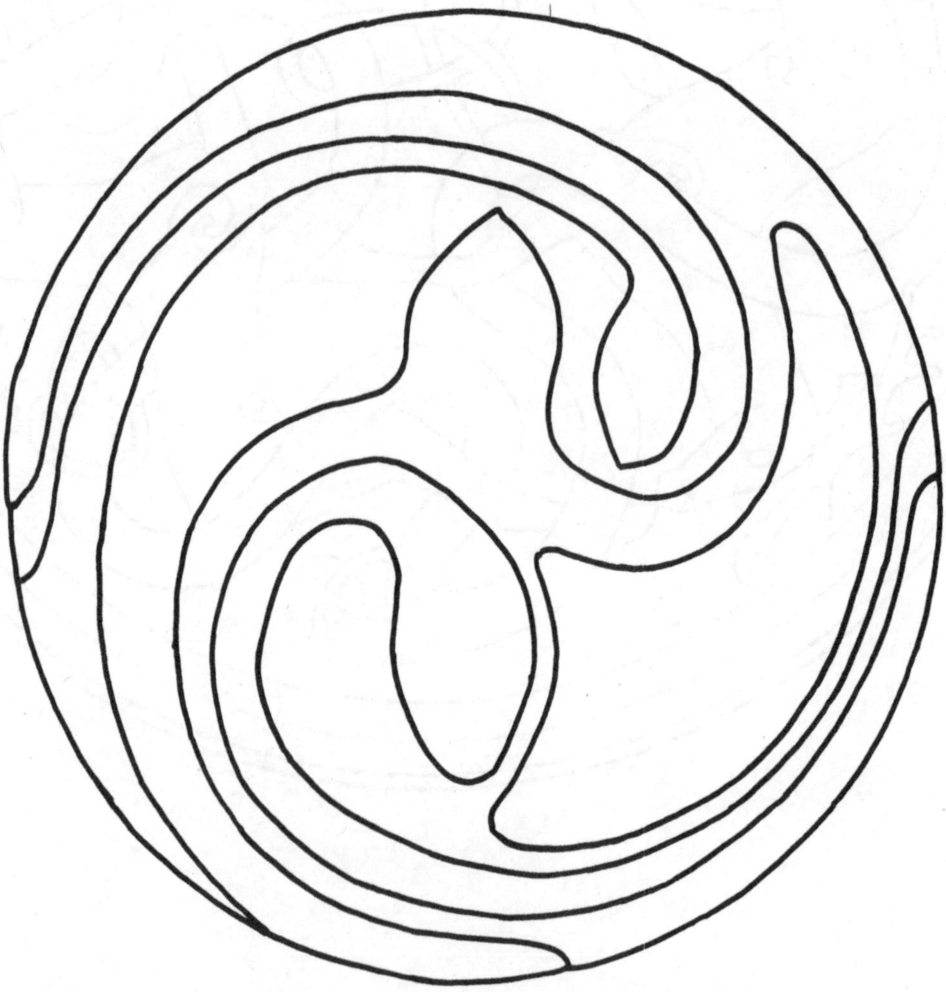